Contents

Emotional Intelligence Explained:

How to Master Emotional Intelligence and Unlock Your True Ability

By C.K. Murray

Happiness comes through emotions qualified by the heart.
Doc Childre

~~~~~~~~~~

It's true you know, what they say. If you can conquer your emotions, you can conquer your life. And why wouldn't you? Why wouldn't you learn to master those 'things' that matter most—the feelings that *guarantee* true success?

Humans are creatures of emotion, not logic. Everywhere we go, emotions are swirling. When we're in a hurry at the checkout, but the cashier doesn't care because she's stuck there for another 6 hours. When we're meeting that special somebody for the first date, our heart throbbing and our mind reeling.

Or how about those hours and minutes prior to your big moment? When the pit in your stomach and the voice in your head scream—"don't mess this thing up!"

Learning to deal with emotions is *indispensable* to healthy and happy living. Some people become slave to their emotions, crumbling when times are rough and likewise losing their heads when times are good. Heck, some people can't even *begin* to understand the feelings in their hearts.

For some of us, life is a perpetual battle between our thoughts and feelings. But this is only part of the problem, because emotional intelligence is more than just understanding ourselves. Emotional intelligence is a *pervasive* power. It's the ability to understand others as well; to work with others, exist with others, live with others, adapt to others—and change others—in a way that changes our *own* lives for the better.

Without emotional intelligence, we're screwed. You could be the biggest braniac in the world, but if you don't have a grip on your emotions and the emotions of others, good luck succeeding! Put simply, we all stand to gain from emotional intelligence. And if you think you know, think again.

For now, let's review the basics. Then we'll get to the more interesting stuff.

What is Emotional Intelligence?

Firstly, this begs the question: what is intelligence?

To put it in general terms, intelligence is the ability to learn or understand things and situations, old and new. When it comes to *emotional* intelligence, this ability has to do with, well, emotions. But emotional intelligence is a little more complex than this.

In 1997, psychologists John Mayer and Peter Salovey founded the theory of emotional intelligence. In their words, such intelligence encapsulated the ability "to perceive emotions, to access and generate emotions so as to assist thought, to understand emotions and emotional knowledge, and to reflectively regulate emotions so as to promote emotional and intellectual growth."

But it didn't end there. As it turned out, emotional intelligence would come to encompass a *wide* range of relevant skills, perceptions, and behavioral responses.

Nowadays, emotional intelligence constitutes four main areas of competence. For most of us, these areas are underdeveloped. They include:

Self-Sentience

Sentience refers to awareness. When we are fully sentient of ourselves, we readily recognize how our emotions affect our thoughts and behaviors. Beyond this, we recognize that we are by no means perfect—both strengths and weaknesses come together to create who we are and how we feel. As a result of this awareness, we are better able to appraise ourselves accurately and confidently.

Self-Regulation– This refers to the ability to monitor our changing feelings, especially strong impulses. Self-regulation allows us to adapt to our changing inner landscape in positive fashion. We take steps to better ourselves, we adhere to our goals and visions, and we modify ourselves at times when modifying our environments is not an option. Managing our emotions in a healthy way ensures that our lows are never too low and our highs never too high. Life can be a rollercoaster sometimes, but when we're self-regulated, we *never* fall off.

Social-Sentience

The power of emotional intelligence often comes from one's awareness of others. If you can understand the emotions, concerns, needs and wants of other people, you can readily adapt to novel situations. Detecting subtle emotional changes, picking up on cues, and recognizing the dynamics of any group or collective are critical skills. By fostering these skills, an individual can dramatically improve his or her chances of feeling comfortable in *any* social situation.

Relational Regulation

This is one of the toughest areas to master. No matter who you are or what you do, relationships will be a factor. When we can regulate and manage our relationships, we gain a power advantage. We learn to communicate clearly, we become influential and inspirational, we function well in groups, and we gain the ability to manage problems. In the end, relational regulation allows us to climb the ladder of success in what is a very socially-connected modern world.

How Does Emotional Intelligence Affect Us?

Put bluntly, emotions are everything.

People who are knowledgeable or smart aren't going to succeed if they can't coexist with others. If they are not *socially-sentient*, they end up alienated and isolated. If they are not *self-sentient*, they end up sabotaging themselves at every turn. If they fail to regulate themselves and their relationships, they will never go anywhere.

Emotional intelligence has a significant impact on:

Relationships

As social creatures, human beings need to have relationships to survive. We are brought into this world by caregivers. We are nurtured and molded by role models and guardians. And as we age, the emotions of others become central factors in our own lives. Whether at work, at home, or simply in day-to-day interactions, emotional intelligence warrants a firm grasp of relationships. A high emotional intelligence will allow you to feel and understand how others feel in order to communicate clearer, form stronger bonds, and enjoy a socially successful life.

And if you like being a 'lone wolf,' don't take things too far. Healthy social relationships have been shown to extend life by <u>slowing cognitive decline</u>.

Work Performance

Every office or workplace has its politics. Learning how to work your way through the fluff and get to the top is going to require a strong awareness of yourself and others. Emotional intelligence allows you to inspire others, impress your superiors, and lead your inferiors. Many companies nowadays actually assess emotional intelligence through standardized tests!

So forget about needing emotional intelligence to succeed at your job or career. You need emotional intelligence just to *get* a job or career.

Physical Wellbeing

Remember, emotional intelligence requires that you learn to adapt to your darkest days and brightest hours. If you're unable to control yourself at either extreme, you could end up damaging yourself. Not to mention, the inability to manage emotions diminishes one's ability to harness stress positively. If we don't control our psychological stress, many of our bodily functions can go haywire.

Firstly, there's blood pressure. There are plenty of natural ways to reduce hypertension, but when our emotions are left unchecked, we often forget to act rationally. Which means we forget to do the smart things that are good for us. What happens in the end is that we actually worry, work, or exercise ourselves sick. We weaken our immune systems, increase the risk of heart attacks and strokes, increase the likelihood of fertility problems, and ultimately end up aging *way* too early.

Hate grey hair, thinning hair, wrinkles, aches, pains, discomforts, diseases, illnesses, and everything bad? Good, then get your emotions in check!

Mental Wellbeing

They say that your body and mind are connected, and this could never be more true than for emotional intelligence. Unharnessed stress often leads to a variety of psychological issues such as depression, anxiety, suicidal ideation, neurosis, obsessive compulsive behavior, and self-destruction. The inability to understand and manage emotions can cause mood swings, perpetuating feelings of isolation and worthlessness. At the very least, low emotional intelligence results in lack of success. At the very worst, lack of emotional intelligence can lead to psychosis and even death.

All these things said, emotional intelligence can easily be raised. If we can learn to harness stress, maintain focus, and sustain an inner and outer connection, then we can learn to change. By resolving conflicts positively, using humor in tough circumstances, employing effective nonverbal communication, and responding rationally to emotions, we are well on our way to boosting EQ.

But before we can boost EQ, we need to know what it is. That is to say, how does one measure EQ?

Sure, you've heard of Intelligent Quotient (IQ) tests that require us to solve problems, match words, find patterns and the like.

But how the heck do tests measure *Emotional* Quotient?

Measuring Your Emotions: EQ VS IQ

The debate about intelligence has been going on for a long time. Some people define intelligence as performance on standardized tests. Others claim that there are multiple types of intelligences, while some still think that intelligence is a fluid and unquantifiable concept.

When it comes to the commonly accepted intelligence score, most specialists will point to IQ scores, or Intelligent Quotient scores. Although these scores do accurately represent how an individual performs on a certain type of test, many argue that this measure is too narrow to encompass the depth and breadth of human ability.

Like IQ, one's Emotional Quotient (EQ) is typically measured under testing conditions. These tests measure an individual's capability to perceive, control, evaluate, and express emotions. However, there are some critical differences. Although experts still disagree over the extent to which environment and genetics affect IQ, EQ seems to be more fluid. That is to say, one's IQ is more fixed, and one's EQ is more susceptible to change through training.

This is why schools have instituted Social and Emotional Learning (SEL) programs to teach students emotional skills. In certain educational institutions, these programs are actually mandatory parts of the curriculum. Needless to say, social and emotional learning constitute a very important part of development.

Before the concept of EQ came about, IQ was considered the end-all and be-all of life success. By and large, IQ was believed to open doors for anybody. If you had a high one, you were supposed to do well in school, you were supposed to get a good job, and make lots of money, and live a healthier and happier life overall.

Of course, this is simply not true.

Sure, being highly intelligent will make some things easier, but it can also make a lot of things more complicated. We probably all know of at least one girl or guy who seemed to have all the brains, but did nothing with it. For every smart, hard-working kid who went to a great school and got a great degree, there is an equally smart kid who slacked off, dropped out, or altogether shut down any attempt at success. Some of the smartest people do nothing to show it; they suffer in quiet, geniuses with no direction and clue. Although IQ results tell them that they should have the world in their fingers, this couldn't be further from the truth. Maybe they're stuck at a mediocre job, maybe they're depressed or drunk or addicted to drugs.

The bottom line is simple: all their intellectual power could not overcome their lack of emotional power. And this is why emotional intelligence is so important.

And the world knows it's important. Companies assess you based on your emotional intelligence. Leadership potential typically relates to higher EQs, so big corporations will make sure you have what it takes.

The good news is, EQ can be raised through training and courses. Meta-analyses reveal that roughly half of students in SEL classes perform better on achievement tests and some 40% improve their GPAs. Higher emotional intelligence has also been linked to reduced suspension rates, improved attendance rates, reduced disciplinary issues, reduced job tardiness, reduced absenteeism, increased productivity, improved upward mobility and increased job security.

So if you're wondering where you fit in, and don't want to take some phony online test, look no further. The following standardized instruments will give you a good idea of your EQ:

Reuven Bar-On's EQ-i

This one is a self-report test that measures competencies such as awareness, stress resistance, problem solving, and happiness. This instrument assesses intelligence as an array of noncognitive capabilities, competencies, and skills that allow one to succeed in different environments.

Multifactor Emotional Intelligence Scale (MEIS)

This is scale is similar to some IQ tests administered to young children. In other words, it asks test-takers to perform tasks. Instead of being strictly question-based, this examination makes the examinee actively interact with changing environments to assess the ability to perceive, identify, understand, and utilize emotions.

Seligman Attributional Style Questionnaire (SASQ)

This one measures optimism and pessimism, weighing

one's perceptions in order to determine potential for emotional coping. The SASQ is probably the most deviant from core emotional intelligence testing.

Emotional Competence Inventory (ECI)

The ECI relies not on a test-taker's abilities, but on the reports of family members and friends of the assessed individual. These individuals offer ratings over a variety of emotional competencies. This may be a good alternative for those who feel that self-reports like the Reuven Bar-On's EQ-I are biased. Of course, depending upon the opinion of those offering the ratings, an examinee may be rated significantly higher or lower than expected.

Once you've measured your EQ formally or informally, you are ready for the next step. In knowing where you stand, you stand to improve. You can identify areas of weakness and draw confidence from your strengths. And if you find that you're weak in literally *every* category of EQ, there is no need to worry!

Social and Emotional Learning (SEL) courses are just one way to improve emotional intelligence. You can also improve by making real-world changes on a daily basis.

So let's start! There are virtually unlimited ways to boost your EQ. Whether seeking to climb the corporate ladder, improve relations with those that matter, feel more comfortable in social situations, exude a powerful charisma, relieve stress, improve mood, or simply find happiness in everyday moments, Emotional Intelligence is your gateway.

Here we go!

What are Soft Skills?

One area where emotional intelligence is *critical* is the workplace.

In today's uncertain economic times, qualifications and performance are only part of the equation. Although any company will value an employee with the know-how and results to prove it, these qualities can only go so far. In fact, Forbes magazine now cautions *all* workers, part-time or career, to think outside the box. Instead of focusing merely on skillsets specific to the job, employees must cultivate those other, less tangible, equally-as-important skills.

These skills are called "soft skills" and incorporate a variety of emotional competencies. Basically, soft skills are the opposite of hard skills. So-called hard skills are the easily defined abilities you must possess to work for a given company. You can probably think of some of them off the top of your head. Knowledge and experience with systems, experience with certain products or services, experience with performing tasks and chores. Maybe it's bartending, maybe it's knowing how to use Microsoft software, maybe it's knowing construction supplies, or engineering, or cosmetology. When you have a hard skill that a company is seeking, you generally know it. When you don't have that skill, or experience, you generally know it as well.

However, when we are lacking soft skills, we might be clueless. Soft skills are not always so obvious. Soft skills are people skills; soft skills are self-management skills. They are that all-too-important and all-too-subtle bundle of personality traits, social talents, communication skills, habits, attitudes and feelings that make us successful.

And when it comes to reaching new levels of success, nothing is more important than *accelerating* your career through the right soft skills.

Top Soft Skills to Accelerate Your Career

We've all seen them or know them. They're the go-getters. The smooth talkers. The guys and gals that seem to have it all; an ease to their words, and a confidence to their walk. They might not always be the best or the brightest, but when it comes to saying the right thing, their words are always on target.

These are the deal-sealers. They're the businessmen and women who can understand the client before the client opens his mouth. They're the menial day-laborers, getting by on minimal work by winning their bosses' sense of humor. These are the people in all jobs and careers that know how to act and when to act it. When it comes to people, *these* people know the game. And though they might not work as hard or have as much technical experience, they've *always* got a leg up.

So how do they do it?

Well, the simple answer is mastery. These emotional geniuses have learned how to take the most critical soft skills and take the reins. They don't sweat the small stuff and they don't drain their minds pouring over the books. What they know, more than anything else, is playing politics. They know that 85% of financial success is based on human connectivity; only 15% is based on technical knowledge. IQ counts for only 10-25% of success.

And when it comes to success, no soft skills matter more than these:

Empathy

It doesn't matter if you're a budding entrepreneur or a cashier at Wendy's. If you have empathy you can better relate to your customers, clients, coworkers and superiors. Empathy is about more than simply showing compassion or sympathizing for somebody else. Empathy is a skill tuned through *vicarious* experience. In other words, we cultivate empathy when we relate to somebody who is important to us. It might be our boss or it might be an important customer. By empathizing, we temporarily take on another person's feelings and allow them to pass through us.

In order to cultivate empathy in everyday situations, it is wise just to listen. So many people don't know how to listen. When you truly listening, you're not just hearing what somebody else has to say. You're taking it in, you're allowing it to integrate with your own ideas and past experiences. When we listen, we welcome the feelings and emotions expressed by another person. Not only do we hear the words, we hear the tone, the loudness, the pitch, the facial expressions and body language that characterize those words. Simply by listening more and talking less, we can really begin to unearth the power of empathy. We can even further this by asking interested questions, by really delving deep into why the person feels a certain way, or what a person is really thinking.

Once we have empathized to a certain extent, we begin to make the amends that are necessary. We realize that empathy prepares us for all future work interactions. Think about it. If you know how your boss feels or typically feels, you can respond in ways that impresses him or her. If you can develop empathy with your coworkers, they will not only respect and trust you, they will come to see you as caring and open-minded leader. And if you can empathize with a client or customer, you significantly increase your chances of closing a deal, making a sale, selling a service, building rapport, getting return business—you name it.

Empathy is key!

Bargaining

Now don't think that bargaining only refers to negotiations in the business world of sales. Bargaining can refer to even the most simple matters at any 9-5 job. Say, for instance, that you want to get time off for vacation, but your boss needs you certain days become somebody else is already requested off. In these cases, you need to know how to bargain—you need to know how to make a deal, or arrangement, that works for you, your boss, and the company. Or, perhaps, you're involved in trying to negotiate your raise, and your superiors are reviewing your performance reviews, and you know that if you don't sway them with the right words, you're screwed.

Heck, bargaining can even refer to wanting to change your hours. Even more, you don't even *have* to have a job to need bargaining skills. When sitting in that job interview, you are essentially selling yourself, as a product to the company. Just as salesmen would try to sell a product by striking a negotiation, you need to strike a negotiation with your potential employer. Why are you better than other applicants? How can you be an asset that will offset any concerns or considerations management sees?

Bargaining is a crucial soft skill and tool that can bring us from no-man's land to success city. When learning to cultivate bargaining, what you do is simple. Firstly, you need to learn how to be a player. You need to play the game according to the rules. And the rules are brief.

(A) Preparation – come with all your paperwork, proof, support, evidence. Make sure all your reasons for your position are worked out logically in your head and on paper if need be. Know what you need to say and why, and know how you will respond to expected questions or inquiries.

(B) Flexibility—You might not get what you want. That, after all, is the story of life. If you don't get the terms you want, have an alternative set up. Make sure that it is the best alternative you can think of. It should find a middle ground that gives the other party something to bite into, just as it gives you that little something that *you* seek. When presenting this alternative, be firm, be assertive, and be respectful. Show how it helps both of you, and explain matter-of-factly how you are more than happy to give up your first position in favor for this lesser, but acceptable, alternative.

C) Stay Rational—Remember, no matter what happens, stay rational. Don't allow your emotions to run away from you. Even if your boss, coworker, or subordinate is totally out of control, make sure that you are not. Make sure that you are the one who is reasoned and intelligent. If the other party reacts with strong emotion, counter that emotion with reason. Few things defuse strong emotion better than a steady, calm voice and a strong belief. Don't overuse body language or facial expressions. Keep your eye contact firm and your chin up. Don't allow the tone of your voice to fluctuate. Don't overuse gestures. Make your hand gestures firm and repetitive. Don't overstate yourself. Repeat calmly and confidently your position and express that all parties have something to gain from it.

Communication

Communication skills are integral to success in all facets of life, but especially in the business world. When cultivating this skill, it is important to work it with everybody. Talk to you coworkers about the day's tasks, duties or group projects. Coordinate with others by assuming the leadership. Be the first to recognize problems and quickly bring them to others' attention.

When it comes to business presentations, be sure that you prepare for the unexpected. Knowing Powerpoint is a plus, sure, but you should also be prepared to do most of the talking on your own. Communication is more than just reading off things from a chart or presentation.

Communication is about actively integrating information with your own beliefs, feelings, thoughts, and experiences. Absorb information and make it your own.

Learn how communication changes. You talk differently to your boss than to your coworker. The more you talk to people, the easier it becomes. Not to mention, the more relaxed your workplace cohorts will feel around you.

Practice in a mirror. Imagine talking to somebody at work, in a meeting, at the water-cooler, on lunch break, during a performance review, about an upcoming task, job, project. Imagine asking for time off, negotiating raises, promotions, etc. Begin at the workplace with small talk. Intersperse friendly interactions with business related talk: "how are x, y and z going?" "Should we get to a, b and c?" "Have you started on d, e and f?"

Establishing Rapport

Building a workplace rapport or relationship is impacted by many factors. Firstly, the previous soft skills are all very important. You need to empathize, you need to negotiate and you need to communicate.

You also need to sell yourself. In the business world, where people can get quite sleazy in their self-promotion, 'selling' yourself is quite important. Just don't do it like others. Be sure to stand out by not seeming desperate. Invest in a good business card design, carry around resumes, or even wear a shirt related to your workplace or business. Don't force anything on anybody. Be sure to show genuine interest in others' problems. Offer to help them before you ever ask for them to help you.

Don't overplay your hand like a giddy entrepreneur drooling over that one potential investor. Instead, invest in the long-term approach. Help others and mention what you do and how you aspire to do more. Once you have shown that you are a caring, selfless individual, proceed to the next step. Casually slip them your business card and tell them to contact you if they ever "need anything." Put the emphasis on "need anything," so it seems that you don't want anything but to help them. Put in their mind that *they* are the ones who need *you*, not the other way around.

Use this approach with a variety of other businessmen and women. Always stress that you are the asset and the one willing to help. Too many people get too eager, and they'll inadvertently communicate that they want a favor or "need" something. What this does is subordinate. It puts you in a lower position of power and exhibits lack of self-confidence. Even if you work at McDonalds and haven't ever made more than minimum wage, act as if you have all the ability in the world. If you're handing in your resume, ask to see the head boss, and if he or she is not available, request another manager. If you have no choice but to hand it to a lower-level worker, ask who will be receiving it and communicate that you can't wait to hear back. Be courteous, get the person's name and thank them personally.

Remember, word of mouth spreads like wildfire in the business world. Good performances are great, sure, but often it's the likable employees who get the promotion over the more productive, less personable ones.

Guidance

Guidance is about being a leader. It's about helping others achieve their best. It's about helping yourself achieve your best. It's about taking the faculties you've cultivated, and channeling them in a positive manner to propel everybody forward.

It doesn't matter what your job may be. Even people working as cashiers at Target have to learn how to guide. They guide 'newbs' who are learning the register. They guide coworkers through long, hectic shifts with words of encouragement, by leading through example, by keeping a calm face and a quick swipe in the face of super impatient lines of shoppers.

When becoming a master of guidance in the business world, it's all about knowing people. You need to understand what motivates certain people. To lead others, you need to know others. Some people will respond to stern demands. Others will shrivel up and underperform. You need to notice how others react in terms of productivity, in terms of body language, attitude, response—etc.

When it comes to guiding entire teams to success, it's important to work both collectively and individually. Having group meetings will help but so too will discussing with each member one on one. Establish that rapport and make it stick. Learn what others want out of their job and understand how those goals meet with company goals.

In the end, guiding others—whether at a convenience store or a large conglomerate—is all about inspiration. You need to use positive reinforcement to keep others involved. You need to offer small words of praise, perks such as coupons or discounts or increased lunch time, promotions—you name it. However, when workers don't perform to their standards, the leader must also learn to drop the hammer. Always use constructive criticism. Highlight what somebody is doing well while showing how they can improve. *Never* tell an employee that he or she is doing perfectly, and never tell an employee that he or she is doing everything poorly. Find something good and something bad, and communicate that these are not related to the individual's character or personhood. Relate that job performance is based on effort not ability, and that by working harder and having the right attitude, one can achieve his or her dreams.

To guide, you must motivate. And to motivate, you must awaken in each unique person a drive that he or she never knew existed. What it takes is consistent effort, willingness to fail, and the knowledge that all people want to succeed—no matter their attitude or apparent desire.

Time Organization

You don't have to be a guru to make this happen. And you don't have to obsessively schedule every minor event in your life either. Time organization is simply about attitude. If you have a goal, make a plan. Oftentimes, we start doing something and we're not sure exactly what we're doing. We know we have a vague goal or vision, but we're not sure how to get there. We learn as we go, and the further or farther we go, the more the plan presents itself.

If you like to see things in writing, by all means chart your progress. Or maybe just keep the record playing in your head, so that every day you awake with a clear vision of success. Having concrete goals and an evolving plan is what makes business success and general life success. It gives us priorities and purpose; it makes us happy. It allows us to rest our heads on the pillow at night knowing that we did something useful and can drift off to sleep.

If you want to get ahead of the next guy or gal in the world of business, you need to be productive. But more than that, you need to be specific. Make a habit of allotting certain chunks of your day to high-priority tasks. Allow yourself to focus solely on these projects. Cut off social networks, phones, tablets, and sensory distractions. Put yourself in an environment where stimuli is restricted, where you won't be tempted to think of or engage in other things.

The hardest part is taking that first step. Once you get rolling, you pick up steam and you keep doing it. Once you have successfully scheduled successive chunks of 'productive time,' you will begin to notice a pattern. You'll realize your routine and know how to keep it going.

And remember, save the truly menial stuff for those low-priority hours. Don't waste your high-priority time running to get office supplies when you could delegate somebody else to do it. Instead of worrying excessively about the details, focus on pursuing the high-value goals. Contact customers or clients who offer the most profit potential. Approach angles of a project that pose the biggest roadblock first, and sweat the small stuff later. After all, the old adage rings true: 80% of our business comes from 20% of our customers. Worry about the lesser stuff less. Spend those high-priority hours working hard for the big fish, and blow off steam in the other hours.

Don't be afraid to relax. Relaxation is not laziness. It is a deliberate decision to allow your brain the restoration it needs. Running out of ideas or getting foggy? Give yourself some down-time. Ironically, nothing gets the creative juices flowing better than thinking about nothing.

So there you have it, some of the top soft skills that can elevate your career and shoot you to the top of the world. You don't have to do anything but stay confident and work hard. If you apply the aforementioned skills, you are going to make it happen. Your EQ will give you the abilities you need to overcome even the most blatant failings.

But if you're still skeptical, and still feel as if you're lacking the goods to make it happen, fear no more. Having emotional intelligence extends far beyond career success. A high EQ can open doors that you never even knew existed.

And once you have mastered the art of emotional intelligence, your power will reach entirely new levels.

Enter: *Emotional Resonance…*

Emotional Resonance—Influencing Others to Get What You Want

What is emotional resonance you ask?

Simple, emotional resonance is the way emotions—whether yours or someone else's—are mutually *felt*. When something 'resonates,' it is said to carry a certain quality. With emotions, resonance is about experiencing something as if we can physically touch it. We can feel it deep in our core, undeniably real. It can be powerful and subtle all at once. It is a charisma, an aura, a pervasive power that emanates from the individual and infiltrates our emotional landscape almost effortlessly.

If you've ever been around somebody particularly important, or scary, or just plain different—you've felt it. Emotional resonance gives us meaning. When we say something resonates with us, we mean that we really get it. It *speaks* to us; it's somehow special.

Resonance can help us:

Influence others

Communicate ideas and thoughts

Impress others

Captivate men and women

Implant false beliefs

and

Subordinate others

All this is nice and dandy, but if we don't know how to channel emotional resonance, we're just as powerless as the next guy. So don't be powerless. Take control of your life!

Here's how to maximize your emotional resonance, in every situation. Here's how to influence others <u>today</u>:

Emanate Confidence

Confidence is the gateway to success. If people see that you are confident in your own skin, they will respect you. Your aura will put others at ease and allow them to feel secure. They will be inspired by you; they will be empowered by you. They will feed off your energy and always want more.

Confident people exude positivity. They are happy with who they are, where they're going, and what they're becoming. They don't speak in cynical or negative terms. They don't begin interactions with criticisms, or insults, or self-hatred. Confident people have a zest that they carry wherever they go. It doesn't have to come out in loud words or exaggerated motions. But it is certainly present. Others can see it in their eyes, the lack of fear and belief in ability. Confident people have a positive outlook because they *expect* good results.

Confident people speak confidently. Confident people don't have to yell or speak quickly. They don't have to boast or shout or compare others to themselves in critical ways. Confident people speak deliberately, they speak honestly; they speak in a way that is true to themselves. They don't try endlessly to appease others, and they don't rush through their thoughts to make way for others. Confident people speak with varying tones, pitches, loudness and intonations. Even if they don't always talk, when they do, people listen.

Confident people strive for improvement. Truly confident people take pleasure in who they are, what they do and how they act. They don't stare in the mirror for hours on end, or worry about small pieces of their physical appearance, or constantly contact others for self-esteem boosts. Truly confident people are not internally weak. They acknowledge their shortcomings and strive to change them. They keep their eyes on the prize by always focusing on self-improvement. They are not afraid to fail and not afraid to admit that they are wrong. Making mistakes does not mean that they are incapable. It means that they are learning, and growing, and becoming the best version of themselves that they can be.

Master Your Body Language

Body language actually has the capacity to change the very neurochemical properties of your brain. With the right body language, others will want to be around you. They will want to follow you. Men and women will place trust in you, hanging on your words, and agreeing with you when their logical brain tells them not to.

This is because body language plays on our emotions.

The right body language shows charisma, confidence, and the ability to succeed. The wrong body language tells people that you are unapproachable, weak, uncertain, and incapable of making sense of this world.

Consider some of the basic traits of a master of body language. A master will show confidence by standing tall with the chin tilted up, the eyes straight ahead, the shoulders pulled back, and steady, meaningful strides. Confident people walk with a purpose and swing their arms. They are calm but purposeful. When they enter an unfamiliar place, they do not shrivel into a corner. They look around, they make eye contact, and they search for opportunities to engage.

Confident people have good posture. They don't sit rigidly or loose and floppy. They keep their back straight and their core firm. They deliver firm handshakes that communicate that they mean business. They don't fidget, they don't keep their hands by their faces, they don't avoid eye contact, or face away from people with whom they are interacting. Confident people display open body language, indicating that they are willing to embrace whatever may come their way. They smile genuinely upon meeting somebody new. Their speaking is not rushed, their gestures are firm and consistent, neither rushed nor thrown in randomly. When they talk, they do not lose their voice or waver.

Confident people are not in a hurry to impress others. Others are in a hurry to impress *them*.

When others see this body language, it says one thing: "I'm secure with who I am. Are you?"

Make Others Feel Unique

The power of the *resonant* individual comes from his or her ability to make others feel special. When interacting with others—whether it be a big-time politician or a cashier at the grocery store—resonant individuals use charm. This ability to charm hinges on the individual's ability to speak to *anybody*. If you can speak to anybody, you can say whatever you want whenever you want to.

You can adapt to novel situations, and use that charm to get out of situations where you're clueless.

Making others feel unique is accomplished by:

Acting Equal. Respect others as equal, and expect them to do the same for you. Don't put anybody on a haughty pedestal, and don't treat anybody like dirt. Be respectful of other people, whether they're coworkers, acquaintances, investors, employers, or young students.

Be Interested. Don't poke or prod, but definitely inquire as to the details of others' lives. Show that you care about how things have gone for them, how they're progressing. Communicate that you value their thoughts and feelings, and that your own thoughts and feelings are similar. Don't act as if you don't care.

Listen, don' hear. Don't sit or stand there passively when somebody is telling you something. Instead, show that you are connecting by nodding and saying things like, "Okay," "I got you," or "I see." Give brief contact such as shoulder touches or hand touches to physically connect yourself to the other person. Hold eye contact, and ask follow-up questions. Be involved.

Remember, remember. A resonant individual will remember faces *and* names. If you are bad at remembering names, try effective mnemonics. Once you have catalogued a list of people, be sure to always address them by name. Offer genuine compliments and be nice because you want to be, not because you feel you have to be. Take compliments graciously and don't make a deal of them. Know that you are a charismatic, compliment-worthy person. Know that you are awesome!

Master Wit

A truly resonant person will learn how to master the art of wit. This individual will employ humor and charisma in tandem, drawing upon various circumstances and situations in order to make others laugh. People love to laugh, and anybody who can lighten the load and make life seem less serious is a person that others want to be around. A truly resonant person will poke fun at him or herself without seeming insecure or self-loathing. The ability to show comfort with one's own flaws is a powerful tool. To fully master your wit, you should strive to:

> Learn the Dynamics. If you're around a bunch of 'prudes,' certain jokes simply won't fly. However, if you're in a group of people who like crude or dirty jokes, feel free to give it a stab. If you do happen to overstep your bounds, show that you recognize it, and poke fun at your obvious cluelessness. Always,

always start conservatively until you've discovered another person's boundaries. It's better to go slow than to offend a person right off the bat. Stay attuned and keep at it; eventually, others will see you as a comfortable and versatile person.

Don't overdo it. You don't have to be a standup comedian. In fact, if you crack too many jokes, nobody will take you seriously, and then you'll lose the ability to influence them in serious matters. Instead, focus on context-appropriate jokes, and use them sparingly. Be funny when the mood is lighthearted. Focus on quality, not quantity.

Become Engrossing

Beyond simply being funny, charismatic and confident, the resonant individual is engrossing. In other words, the resonant individual is a person who draws in others. To become more engrossing, one should:

Learn! One should be well-read, knowledgeable and stimulated. One should read newspapers, magazines, journal articles, blogs, twitter—etc. Anything to increase knowledge of things that matter like worldly events, science, sociology, humankind, and important historical touchstones. The point is not to know a lot about something, but to know a *little* about everything. This allows for an individual to enter conversations at whim and feel confident. The resonant person is not an expert; he or she is simply widely informed.

Think First. Cut down on small talk and meaningless fluff. Organize your thoughts before expressing them, and if you have something to say,

say it with conviction. Don't feel as if you have to say something just to say something. The less you speak, the more gravity your words hold. Especially if they're well thought-out.

Open Up. People will find you engrossing if you are willing to put your emotions out there in honest fashion. If they hear you speaking and acting in a respectable manner, they will appreciate who you are. You can have strong emotions but still express them tactfully. Do so and keep the feelings of others in consideration. If others see that you have a strong, well-reasoned stance, they'll want to know why. And before you know it, they'll want to know *everything* about you.

Well there you have it. A *resonant* person is a person who captivates others. A resonant person possesses a repertoire of conversational skills, social graces, body gestures, and emotional abilities. A resonant person is the type of person that others want to follow and understand; the type of person that makes other men and women inferior—in a way that is neither disrespectful nor blatant.

But sometimes being resonant is not enough. Even for the resonant individual life can be tough. Sometimes, no matter what we do or think, the walls seem like they're closing in.

And if you've ever struggled with a relationship, with keeping your feet on the ground and your heart open—you *know*. You know what it's like to struggle, over time, through thick and thin, with a weakening relationship.

Which is why Emotional Intelligence becomes paramount *yet again*…

How to Communicate Your Feelings in EVERY Relationship

Communication is the foundation of every healthy relationship.

Think about it. When you're with your friends, your family, coworkers or acquaintances—it doesn't matter. No matter who you're with or why, the ability to effectively convey thoughts, feelings, and attitudes is critical. And it doesn't even have to be verbal. Over 90% of communication is nonverbal. How we portray ourselves and project our emotions says a lot about who we are. It says what we want and need, and why we want and need it.

Without effective communication, without the ability to convey those all-important feelings, relationships suffer. And this is no surprise. When couples stop communicating, they grow apart. When you stop contacting or seeing your friends, you feel distant. When we fail to engage others in general, things just feel off. We lose track of ourselves, we get more anxious, depressed, unsure of what we're doing. Isolation ensures. And in the end, our emotions take over.

Say goodbye to happy, healthy living.

Fortunately emotional intelligence can change this. If you're suffering from lack of communication, miscommunication or *too much* communication, your EQ drops. In order to bring it back up and repair estranged or unhealthy relationships, we must all learn to communicate.

Communication adheres

Relationships succeed when communication is placed first and foremost. It is the *adhesive*. It makes everything else— trust, commitment, empathy, compassion—stick together. See, if you can't talk to somebody or at least understand that somebody's emotions, you will never fully trust them. If you can't get your thoughts or feelings across, in some form, you won't commit. If you can't express and/or interpret the emotions involved in a relationship, you simply won't care. After all, you can't show compassion or empathy for somebody you don't *get*. In other words, if there is no connection, then there is nothing. Whether friend, lover, father, mother, son, coworker, or some person you met in Walmart—making connection is key. And the best way to make a connection is through effective communication of our feelings.

Communication changes

No one person will say or express the same emotion in the same fashion. We all have different bodies, tones, expressions, gestures, and manners of speaking. The intensity and frequency of our feelings change depending upon everything around us, and inside us. Everything from what happened at work, where we live, who we date, the current season, the weather, the day of the week, the state of our health—even the kind of food we've put into our body on a given day.

Our emotional states are always changing, coinciding with thoughts, old and new. Which can only mean one thing. Our communication strategies have to adapt. We can't expect to communicate the same way we did with a friend one moment as we do after the death of that friend's father. You can't talk to your ex the same way you two used to when you were dating. We have to be wary of these changes, however subtle, and react accordingly.

Communication defines

They say actions speak louder than words, but why? Can't the two just get along?

See, when it comes to arguments, communication is certainly present. It's just the wrong kind. Constant bickering, fighting and argumentative communication say one thing and one thing only: "We don't understand each other." And it is this label, this branding of our character, that speaks louder than the words that created it.

Like it or not, communication, miscommunication, and lack of communication define us.

Some people are "good listeners." Some people are "bad listeners." There are 'talkers' and 'doers,' people that wear their hearts on their sleeves and people who keep even the smallest emotions buried deep inside. Our bodies, our tones, our history of words and actions all speak to our character. They all communicate an image of who we are.

But whether that image is the one we *want*, is another story…

Which is why effective communication is critical. If you have a desire to mend your relationships, to express your emotions readily and clearly, delay no further! Here is what you <u>need</u> to do:

Understand Your World

This may sound a little odd, but stop and think about it. In today's modern world, we are constantly inundated with data. We process messages and calls and videos and all sorts of electronic bits of information. Amid this maelstrom of incoming stuff, we often lose track of what really matters. Effective communication is about more than just swapping information; effective communication means understanding the emotional basis for that information. It's about reading between the lines, knowing the subtext, seeing the big picture and not just the minute-to-minute details. Effective communication in our relationships enables us to resolve conflict, appreciate differences, establish trust and create flourishing environments where progress and positive emotions can intertwine.

Effective communication allows us to navigate the sometimes confusing world of negative or difficult messages. By cultivating communication through practice, it becomes commonplace. It takes on an automatic quality that imprints upon others.

The more practice we get in, the more powerful and instinctive our communication skills become.

Attention

This is about listening. Listening is a skill that you are probably tired of hearing about at this point, but that's only because it's so important. It's worth repeating, again and again and again. Good listening means understanding how the speaker feels, and not just understanding the words intellectually. The reason that listening is so important is simple: it creates the right environment. This is an environment in which ideas are not attacked or silenced. People can be comfortable; they can share and collaborate. Emotions and thoughts can be discussed, they can be debated, but they can never been destroyed. In this environment, people feel safe and secure in expressing themselves. Negative emotions can be released and relieved, and misunderstandings can be cleared. Creativity is encouraged. Nobody is always right and nobody is always wrong. Some ideas are better than others, but no single idea is without merit. Everybody comes from a different place in life, and for this reason and this reason alone, every idea at least deserves a chance. At the very least, a listen.

So listen! Be sure to:

Give Full Focus

Focus on body language, and other nonverbal communication signals. Looking at your phone, computer, or television is going to make it hard to fully follow what somebody is saying. If you have trouble concentrating on another person, or find them boring, try repeating what they're saying to yourself. Focus on speaking inside you head in an interesting voice. Allow yourself to have a conversation with yourself. Ask why it matters and then reply in the interesting voice. Keep the task of learning fun and creative. Accept that there are always different ideas and beliefs bouncing off one another. Consider how the speaker's words relate to what you know.

Don't Cut-Off

Nothing is worse for listening that an interruption. A lot of people don't listen because they're simply waiting for their turn to talk. Listening isn't about *me, me, me*. It's about caring for what the person is saying and allowing that care to show. If you aren't listening, but instead thinking of what you're going to say, the speaker can usually tell. And if you interrupt the speaker merely to say what you want to say, you definitely aren't listening.

Suspend Judgment

Communication is not about liking somebody. It's about *respecting* them. Even if you don't like somebody, there is no reason not to listen to them. You don't have to agree with somebody's ideas or beliefs to communicate. Remember, suspending judgment can allow you to perceive what somebody is saying. More than that, it allows you to see where that person is coming from, why he or she thinks a certain way, and why he or she acts a certain way. No one person has come from the same background, so don't think that somebody is 'wrong' because his or her experiences don't match with yours.

Be Welcoming

It's always important to welcome the exchange of ideas. Whether small talk or involved intellectual discussion, welcome the comments, replies, and retorts of others. This can be done by smiling, nodding your head and using words such as "really," "uh-huh," "go on," and so on.

Body Language and Nonverbal communication

Everywhere you go and everything you do involves some sort of body language or nonverbal communication. This includes facial expressions, body movement and gestures, eye contact, posture, the way your voice moves, and the way your muscle tension and breathing do their thing. The way you move, appear and act communicates significantly more than what you actually say.

If you want to communicative effectively, understanding body language and nonverbal communication is a must.

Perceive and Perform

Using and recognizing body language is important and not overly difficult. If you want to communicate that you are relaxed and open, keep your posture tall, your chin up, your arms uncrossed, your eyes focused, your legs spread and your arms relaxed at your side. If you want to communicate that you are not open to interaction, do the opposite. Close your body, pull your shoulders in, avoid eye contact, keep your arms crossed, and generally contract your body.

The body language you exhibit depends on your goals and your wants. If you want to get closer to somebody, use physical contact and smiles and touches and pats and hugs. If you want to show that you are sexually attracted, make intermittent eye contact, make subtle body contact, laugh, show your body and show your face.

Just be careful, some body language is not universal. There are numerous cultural differences we need to manage if we wish to effectively communicate.

However, managing body language is also about knowing what to look for. If you can spot certain cues, signals, or even deceptive attempts, you are better positioned for communication success.

To cultivate these skills, practicing being a people peeper. Sit on a bench in a mall or board walk, or just adopt a more observant attitude wherever you go. People on buses, trains, restaurants, stores and T.V. shows often display a variety of telltale signs. Work on comparing what the person says with what the person shows. Try to guess how people feel about each other, the dynamics of relationships, what one person is truly thinking, etc. For fun, attempt to predict how one person will react. One great way to do this is to watch the news on mute, or to wear headphones in a public place with no music. If you can turn off the sound, you'll be amazed how more attuned your other senses become!

Another thing to remember is to acknowledge idiosyncrasies. Not only do people from different cultures and countries use varied nonverbal communication, but certain individuals within the same culture may differ. You have to know the emotional state and baseline of an individual to truly know what he or she is communicating. Some people may have a sad looking face even when they are happy. Some people may constantly furrow their brows, unknowingly, even if they have no feelings of doubt, irritation or the like.

Reading people begins with knowing that person's normal. For instance, certain individuals may put on a big smile to hide the fact that they are really upset. It's all about getting to know the person in question.

It's also important to view body language in 'clusters.' Don't take one gesture or expression and generalize it to all of a person's feelings. Take into consideration everything, including tone of voice, eye contact, gestures, movements and positions. Scratching your eye or diverting your eyes doesn't necessarily mean you're hiding information or being deceitful. Maybe you simply have an itch, or saw something!

When applying body language, make sure to align your nonverbal with your verbal. Imagine what it would be like if somebody always contradicted his or her body language. It would be exhausting trying to decode what the person really meant or felt. So don't be exhausting! If you say you're happy, don't grunt and groan. If you say you agree, don't shake your head. Again, know the body language that is specific to your region or culture. It may differ, and harmless gestures in one location may be severely insulting in others. Adjust to the context and understand that one person, such as an employer, cannot be regarded the same way as your best friend.

Another cool thing you can do is trick your mind. Research shows that body language causes measurable changes in the brain's chemistry. If you are nervous, pulling your shoulders back, straightening your back, keeping your arms at your side and looking ahead will actually make you feel more confident. Doing these things *actually* lower the levels of the stress hormone cortisol. In addition, testosterone levels go up, making for an improved mood. Not to mention, seeming confident and fearless is a good way to put others at ease and get the response you want.

Harnessing Stress

Periods of acute stress are not bad—if we know how to harness them. When stress floods our bodies and brains, we can choose to use that stress to power through important tasks and events, or we can let that stress shut us down and hurt us. The problem with most people is that they don't know how to use stress effectively. They focus so much on its stigmatized qualities that they fail to realize how useful it can be. Moreover, some people become so accustomed to getting stressed, that they don't know how to escape. They allow stress to define them, and in the end, they quickly become people they, and others, resent.

Stress is one of the main reasons for relationship issues. Couples stress over money, children, jobs, interests, time in the day—you name it. Friends stress over not feeling appreciated, valued, acknowledged or included. Relatives and family members and acquaintances and coworkers can all share similar difficulties. The important thing to remember is:

Recognition and Reaction

Stress becomes more powerful the more we feed into it. If we start to worry, "oh my god, oh my god, I'm losing it," we're only going to become more stressed. But if we take the moment to think rationally, then the stress becomes advantageous. The first thing to do is recognize your body's reaction. Don't fight it, just notice it. Is your skin flushed, your pulse up? Are you sweating? Are your teeth or firsts clenched? Do you feel a knot in your stomach? Are you lightheaded?

When communicating, it's important to stop and think. Do you want to continue feeling angry or are you going to calm down first? Realize that you can harness stress by channeling it. Know that you are stressed and use that as a springboard to propel you forward. Don't blow up at somebody. Don't yell or scream. Instead, relate your emotions calmly but firmly. Relax your muscles by clenching and releasing. Take deep breaths, recall a calming memory or image. Take a moment to savor the multi-sensory experience of living, tell yourself that you are ready and capable, and go *tackle* that challenge!

Sometimes humor helps with stress. If you are humorous, you can make anybody feel better. If you see somebody extremely worried or scared, poke fun at something trivial. Explain that you understand the severity while also distracting the person's thoughts from that severity through jokes, witticisms and laughs.

Of course, sometimes humor alone is not enough. In relationships, some people are so firmly stuck in their position that they won't allow even the *hint* of a smile. So don't try to be overly humorous if it is failing. Instead, elect to compromise. Finding a middle ground allows each person to get something. It shows compassion and thought, and naturally controls stress. In the end, if the other party is more emotionally invested in something, it might be best just to let it slide. Relationships are all about give-and-take, and holding onto something just to 'win' is never a good idea. Sometimes, it's simply best to agree to disagree.

Emotional Cognizance

Emotional Intelligence makes or breaks communication. More than the way you think, the way you *feel* will have the impact. If you cannot comprehend your feelings, why they are or what they are, you surely won't be able to communicate them. Ultimately, the inability to understand feelings leads to conflict, separation, and disintegration of meaningful relationships. Think about it. When couples don't resolve underlying emotional breakdowns, they begin to bicker over the smallest things—often things that are far removed from the real problems. They'll argue over leaving the dishes out, not buying enough detergent, leaving the heat too high or the AC too cool—a bunch of silly things that all stem from a failure to communicate.

Effective communication comes from acknowledging and openly discussing emotions. Too many people suppress them or deflect them or numb them through vices like drinking, drugging, eating, gambling, compulsive spending, etc. Too many people fail to realize that a rational approach is good but not enough. Relationships exist on both a rational and emotional level. Ignoring the importance of emotions denies what it is to be human, and prevents further understanding, problem solving, conflict resolution, rapport and intimacy.

When our EQ is high, we learn to approach reality in a productive manner. Emotional intelligence allows us to empathize with others, to understand our troubles, to maintain motivation and optimism, to interact with others of different perspectives, and to build powerful, rewarding relationships that further our lives in positive fashion.

When we communicate effectively, we find that critical balance between intellect and emotions. We know what it takes and we make it happen by being well-adjusted in our approach. Acting purely on emotion means that you never act practically. Acting purely on reason, means that you never feel what yourself or others are experiencing. Success in relationships, and in life, comes from combining both feelings and thoughts. You have to think about something to know what you're truly feeling. And you have to feel something, to know that it exists, before you can rationally think about it.

In short, emotional intelligence in relationships is critical. It keeps us informed and happy. It keeps us in control. We are able to manage extreme emotions like anger, embarrassment, fear, sadness, angst. We are also able to maximize good emotions like joy, pleasure, pride and compassion. Being emotionally intelligent allows us to understand the interplay of thoughts and emotions in ourselves, and in others. And when we master that most delicate interplay, we have mastered the art of communicating.

But sometimes, communicating is just one piece of the puzzle. For many of us, relationships and interactions may go swimmingly. They may be normal and ordinary, neither bad nor good, amazing nor terrible. Even so, something is amiss. Even for people who should otherwise be happy, something seems to be missing. If happiness continues to elude, if you or somebody you know continues to feel as if life should be more positive, more rewarding, more enjoyable—then it's time to act.

Emotional intelligence can bring you happiness like never before...

Feelin' Fine—How to Unlock Personal Happiness through Emotional Smarts

Emotions play a huge part in how we think and behave. If we think we're dumb or worthless, we're going to act that way. We won't take risks, we'll engage in simple, repetitive tasks, we'll lose the will to be versatile, to be excited and challenged and creative. On the other hand, if we feel capable and happy, we'll think that life is full of opportunities. We won't fear failures, we'll tackle challenges, we'll branch out and meet new people and make new friends and try new things. We'll behave positively and proactively, and we'll continue to feed the cycle of a happy, confident lifestyle.

When it comes to these powerful emotions, it's important to recognize what exactly we're dealing with. In dealing with emotions, we must recognize the three primary parts. Firstly, there is the subjective experience, which is how we perceive an emotion. Is it good or bad, strong or subtle? Are we mad or peaceful? Overjoyed or underwhelmed?

Secondly, there is the physiological response to the emotion. Do we feel more energetic because we're happy or do we feel lethargic because we're depressed? Does it move us to action or leave us listless? Does it weaken us or empower us? Hurt us or heal us? Thirdly, is the expressive factor of the emotion. This is tied to the physiological response. How does the emotion affect our behavior towards itself, ourselves, and others? Do we fight it, do we lash out at coworkers and hate ourselves? Do we embrace others, accept our own imperfections, and show more courteous behaviors?

How do we change?

In life, finding happiness is about subjectively experiencing, physiologically responding, and consistently behaving in a manner that fosters positive feelings. It's about taking your emotions and managing them so that you feel better and stronger as a result. Let us remember, emotional health, physical health, and mental health are all intertwined. You can't have one entirely without having at least something of the other. Emotional intelligence improves our health and life by creating:

- A feeling of satisfaction. We are content with where we are and what we're doing. We savor our relationships and our loved ones. We may aspire to achieve something great, but that doesn't mean we're not happy with our current state. We recognize that good things will come, and that where we are now does not define us. Life is a process, and we're damn determined to enjoy every moment.

- A gusto for living. This is about loving and laughing. It's about going out and doing things, kicking back, cracking jokes and loving freedom. It's about being independent and dependable and devilish and kindhearted and spirited and a goofball beyond goofballs. Gusto in life is about embracing the emotional spectrum and never allowing one emotional low or high to rule you. It's about hopping on the rollercoaster and letting the wind blow your hair back. It's about smiling at life's difficulties because, well, who *doesn't* experience them? It's about finding that all-important balance between work and play, rest and activity, and the like. Too much of any one thing will make us unhappy. This is why people with gusto are enthusiastic about *many* things. Love in life's moments—this is where gusto begins.

- Resilience. Again, life can be filled with low moments and negative experiences. For those who have emotional intelligence, resilience keeps them from ever crumbling. If they can manage their emotions, they can stay on top of even the most troubling issues. This can prevent mental and physical deterioration and allow for positive change.

Resilient individuals are smooth sailors by nature—and in the choppy rough we sometimes encounter, this is the best way to survive.

- A life meaning. We can never fully know what we want out of this crazy thing called life till we come to grips with how we feel about things. If we want to feel good, we have to do good. If we want to do good, consistently, we have to feel good. People with a life meaning have looked inward and have looked outward. They have established what they want from life and how they plan to get there. They don't necessarily know the meaning of life, but they do know how they want to go about living it. Life meaning is one of the main factors in personal happiness. Sometimes, it's as simple as knowing the power of the present. Meaning is all around us, in the smallest of details. All we need to do is learn to open our minds.

- Fulfilling relationships. A thriving social network is one of the leading factors in human longevity. Research even shows that having a support network can drastically slow age-related neurodegeneration. But really it's about the quality of friends. Don't be a Facebook junkie and amass 5,000 'friends' you don't know. Instead, opt to find people who are close and understanding. Establish a close circle of confidants who can bring you back from the darkness when life is just too much. Find these people and hold onto them for dear life!

- Self-confidence. Confidence keeps us in control. It means that we don't allow stress to control us. We don't allow others to run over us. We don't shell up at the thought of intimidating people, and we don't shut don't at the thought of messing up or failing.

Self-confidence is about looking in the mirror and seeing something we're proud of. Self-confidence is about <u>unlocking your inner power.</u>

In order to improve Emotional Intelligence for happiness, we need to first understand our relationship with our emotions. Do your experiences flow, with one emotion cascading into another? Are they indistinguishable or can you perceive discrete emotions taking control? Do the emotions come with intense physical sensations? How do you deal with these feelings?

Are you a person that taps into emotions, or that allows them to run over you—or do you try to ignore them altogether? Are there physical problems that you can attribute to your emotions? Do you struggle to sleep? Do you have high blood pressure? Do you experience mood swings, appetite issues, and/or difficulty concentrating? Is your memory filled with negative experiences? Do you struggle to learn new things because you can't clear your head of emotional troubles or obsessions? Do you find that you have so much built up inside of you that you don't know where to start, what to think, or how to express it?

In order to reach happiness, you need to get your emotions in check. This happens by:

- Helping others. Volunteering, opening a door for a disabled person, giving a generous tip, helping somebody at the store, asking a cashier how he or she is doing—all these small things make a positive difference. You don't have to be a philanthropist to make a difference. Simply be positive, be charitable, and be altruistic. Helping somebody and expecting nothing in return is the best way to feel valuable.

- Controlling oneself. Learning how to do things begins by doing them, and sometimes messing up. Fall and get up. Fall and get up. Keep refining your attempts and you'll learn how to do it to the best of your ability. Don't hate yourself for failures. Learn to control your thoughts, emotions and behaviors and you'll be truer to yourself. And once you're true to yourself, you're well on your way to being happy.

- Testing yourself. Nothing makes us feel better than pushing ourselves. Try a new activity, take up regular exercise, get into a board game or hobby that you've always put off. Try thinking activities like neurobics that actually improve your memory, concentration and IQ.

- Getting out in nature. This is one of the reasons that exercise is so important. It gets us out into fields, and forests, out and about where the <u>sun can heal us</u>, where natural aromas improve mental clarity, and where our bodies are meant to be. If you struggle with stress, getting out in nature will help to fight this. Simply walking amid the trees or flowers can extend your life. There are many ways to relax and <u>naturally lower your blood pressure</u>. Not to mention, appealing to the five senses will keep you in a positive mood. Smell flowers, take natural baths, massage yourself, lie on the ground, or sip a nice herbal tea.

- Sustaining creativity. Nothing frees our mind and lifts our heart more than a loved creative outlet. Paint, draw, write, build something in a workshop. Make something that you can call your own, even if you have no intention of ever sharing it. Let out your emotions and you'll be surprised how good you feel.

- Prioritizing the time-out. The time-out refers to any leisure time when you aren't working or busy with everyday obligations. Start doing something because you want to. Even adults need play. Have fun lying in a hammock, going for a hike, walking on a beach, smiling with a friend, reading a book, surfing the web, watching your favorite T.V. show or movie, having sex, eating ice cream, playing a sport. Take time for reflection or deep thought. Think about why you're thankful. Mediate, pray, soak in the skyline, or simply take the time to absorb your surroundings. Don't feel guilty about taking time to just *be*. You deserve it!

Remember, everybody is different. Emotional Intelligence may come easily to some. Just as certain people are naturally better at math or science or language arts, certain people are at a higher starting point in terms of emotions. It's because they come from different backgrounds. They have different motivations and experiences. They've formed different beliefs and opinions, affecting their different feelings and emotions. They can only know what they've seen and felt; however, they can't possibly know, exactly, what *you* have seen and felt.

Don't become disheartened if it takes you a while to boost your emotional intelligence. For some of us, building emotional intelligence is like building a new persona from the ground up. If you have grown up in a family where you were not connected to a primary caretaker, you are at risk for an underdeveloped EQ. You may feel lonely, alienated, confused and beaten down. If you experienced traumas or serious grievances, you are likely to have an underdeveloped EQ. If you have used certain medications, your emotional detection and expression could be off. If you have abused substances, your emotional reasoning could be off. If you have ever experienced severe and personal external or internal issues, your EQ could suffer.

In the end, Emotional Intelligence is all about listening. It's about understanding yourself. It's about understanding others. If you can't come to grips with who you are and how you feel, you will never master emotional intelligence. However, if you continue to fight, to learn, to love and live, then the only limits are the ones you place on yourself. Learn to be happy, learn to control stress, learn to communicate, to empower, to change and conquer. Learn to become the emotional *genius* that you know you can be, and take that critical step toward success.

You can do it!

A Special Note:

Thank you for reading "*Emotional Intelligence Explained: How to Master Emotional Intelligence and Unlock Your True Ability.*" If you enjoyed reading this book and would like to be included on an email list for when similar content is available, feel free:

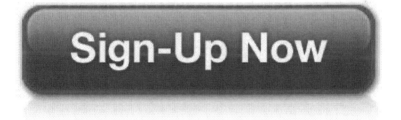

As always, thank you for reading.

And may you continue to live healthily and happily.

Sincerely,

C.K. Murray

Other works by C.K. Murray:

1. *Mindfulness Explained: The Mindful Solution to Stress, Depression, and Chronic Unhappiness*

2. *The Confidence Cure: Your Definitive Guide to Overcoming Low Self-Esteem, Learning Self-Love and Living Happily*

3. *Body Language Explained: How to Master the Power of the Unconscious*

4. *A Reason to Smile: Finding Happiness in Life's Little Moments*

Made in the USA
Columbia, SC
05 September 2024

41865310R00057